For Mother   with Love

From

_____

Date

_____

Published by C.R. Gibson, 32 Knight Street, Norwalk, CT 06856
Designed by Gail Smith
ISBN 0-7667-4844-8
GB524

Text Compilation Copyright © by BBS Publishing Corporation
This edition published by arrangement with BBS Publishing Corporation
Copyright MCMXCVIII C.R. Gibson
Art copyright © Ellen Blonder
All rights reserved.

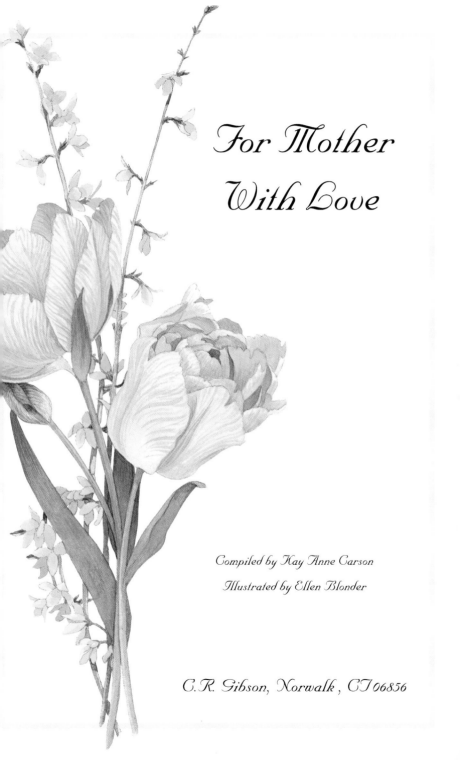

For Mother
With Love

Compiled by Kay Anne Carson

Illustrated by Ellen Blonder

C.R. Gibson, Norwalk, CT 06856

My Mother's Garden

Her heart is like her garden,
Old-fashioned, quaint and sweet,
With here a wealth of blossoms,
And there a still retreat.
Sweet violets are hiding,
We know as we pass by,
And lilies, pure as angel thoughts,
Are opening somewhere nigh.

Forget-me-nots there linger,
to full perfection brought,
And there bloom purple pansies
In many a tender thought.
There love's own roses blossom,
As from enchanted ground,
And lavish perfume exquisite
The whole glad year around.

And in that quiet garden—
The garden of her heart—
Songbirds are always singing
Their songs of cheer apart.
And from it floats forever,
O'ercoming sin and strife,
Sweet as the breath of roses blown,
The fragrance of her life.

Alice E. Allen

Nobody Knows But Mother

How many buttons are missing today?
Nobody knows but Mother.
How many playthings are strewn in her way?
Nobody knows but Mother.
How many thimbles and spools has she missed?
How many burns on each fat little fist?
How many bumps to be cuddled and kissed?
Nobody knows but Mother.

How many hats has she hunted today?
Nobody knows but Mother.
Carelessly hiding themselves in the hay—
Nobody knows but Mother.
How many handkerchiefs willfully strayed?
How many ribbons for each little maid?
How for her care can a mother be paid?
Nobody knows but Mother.

How many muddy shoes all in a row?
Nobody knows but Mother.
How many stockings to darn, do you know?
Nobody knows but Mother.

How many little torn aprons to mend?
How many hours of toil must she spend?
What is the time when her day's work shall end?
Nobody knows but Mother.

How many lunches for Tommy and Sam?
Nobody knows but Mother.
Cookies and apples and blackberry jam—
Nobody knows but Mother.
Nourishing dainties for every "sweet tooth,"
Toddling Dottie or dignified Ruth—
How much love sweetens the labor, forsooth?
Nobody knows but Mother.

How many cares does a mother's heart know?
Nobody knows but Mother.
How many joys from her mother love flow?
Nobody knows but Mother.
How many prayers for each little white bed?
How many tears for her babes has she shed?
How many kisses for each curly head?
Nobody knows but Mother.
Mary Morrison

Huswifery

Make me O Lord, Thy spinning wheel complete.
Thy Holy word my distaff make for me.
Make mine affections Thy swift flyers neat
And make my soul Thy holy spool to be.
My conversation make to be Thy reel
And reel the yarn thereon spun of Thy wheel.

Make me Thy loom then, knit therein this twine:
And make Thy Holy Spirit, Lord, wind quills:
Then weave the web Thyself. The yarn is fine.
Thine ordinances make my fulling mills.
Then dye the same in heavenly colors choice,
All pinked with varnished flowers of paradise.

Then clothe therewith mine understanding, will,
Affections, judgment, conscience, memory,
My words, and actions, that their shine may fill
My ways with glory and Thee glorify.
Then mine apparel shall display before Ye
That I am clothed in holy robes for glory.

Edward Taylor

In An Iridescent Time

My mother, when young, scrubbed laundry in a tub,
She and her sisters on an old brick walk
Under the apple trees, sweet rub-a-dub.
The bees came round their heads, and wrens made talk.
Four young ladies each with a rainbow board
Honed their knuckles, wrung their wrists to red,
Tossed back their braids and wiped their aprons wet.
The Jersey calf beyond the back fence roared;
And all the soft day, swarms about their pet
Buzzed at his big brown eyes and bullish head.
Four times they rinsed, they said. Some things they
starched,
Then shook them from the baskets two by two,
And pinned the fluttering intimacies of life
Between the lilac bushes and the yew:
Brown gingham, pink, and skirts of Alice blue.

Ruth Stone

Easily Given

It was only a sunny smile,
and little it cost in the giving;
But it scattered the night
Like morning light,
And made the day worth living.
Through life's dull warp a woof it wove,
In shining colors of light and love,
And the angels smiled as they watched above,
Yet little it costs in giving.

It was only a kindly word,
And a word that was lightly spoken;
Yet not in vain,
For it stilled the pain
Of a heart that was nearly broken.
It strengthened a fate beset by fears
And groping blindly through mists of tears
For light to brighten the coming years,
Although it was lightly spoken.

It was only a helping hand,
and it seemed of little availing;
But its clasps were warm,
And it saved from harm
A brother whose strength was failing.
Its touch was tender as angels' wings,
But it rolled the stone from the hidden springs,
And pointed the way to higher things,
Though it seemed of little availing.

A smile, a word, a touch,
And each is easily given;
Yet one may win
A soul from sin
Or smooth the way to heaven.
A smile may lighten a falling heart,
A word may soften pain's keenest smart
A touch may lead us from sin apart—
How easily each is given!
Author Unknown

Washing the Dishes

When we on simple rations sup
How easy is the washing up!
But heavy feeling complicates
The task by soiling many plates.

And though I grant that I have prayed
That we might find a serving-maid,
I'd scullion all my days, I think,
To see Her smile across the sink!

I wash, she wipes. In water hot
I souse each dish and pan and pot;
While Taffy mutters, purrs, and begs,
And rubs himself against my legs.

The many who never in his life
Has washed the dishes with his wife
Or polished up the silver plate—
He still is largely celibate.

One warning: there is certain ware
That must be handled with all care:
The Lord Himself will give you up
If you should drop a willow cup!

Christopher Morley

A Child's Grace

Here a little child I stand
Heaving up my either hand;
Cold as paddocks though they be,
Here I lift them up to Thee,
For a benison to fall
On our meat and on us all. Amen.

Robert Herrick

The Reading Mother

I had a Mother who read to me
Sagas of pirates who scoured the sea,
Cutlasses clenched in their yellow teeth,
"Blackbirds" stowed in the hold beneath.

I had a Mother who read me lays
Of ancient and gallant and golden days;
Stories of Marion and Ivanhoe,
Which every boy has a right to know.

I had a Mother who read me tales
Of Gelert the hound of the hills of Wales,
True to his trust till his tragic death,
Faithfulness blent with his final breath.

I had a Mother who read me the things
That wholesome life to the boy heart brings—
Stories that stir with an upward touch,
Oh, that each mother of boys were such!

You may have tangible wealth untold;
Caskets of jewels and coffers of gold.
Richer than I you can never be--
I had a Mother who read to me.

Strickland Gillian

Mis' Smith

All day she hurried to get through
The same as lots of wimmin do;
Sometimes at night her husband said,
"Ma, ain't you goin' to come to bed?"
And then she'd kinder give a hitch,
And pause half-way between a stitch,
And sorter sigh, and say that she
Was ready as she'd ever be,
She reckoned.

And so the years went one by one,
An' somehow she was never done;
An' when the angel said, as how
"Mis' Smith, it's time you rested now,"
She sorter raised her eyes to look
A second, as a stitch she took;
"All right, I'm comin' now," says she,
"I'm ready as I'll ever be,
I reckon."
Albert Bigelow Paine

I Will Make You Brooches

I will make you brooches and toys for your delight,
Of bird-song at morning and star-shine at night.
I will build a palace fit for you and me,
Of green days in forests and blue days at sea.

I will make my kitchen, and you shall keep your room,
Where white flows the river and bright blows the broom,
And you shall wash your linen and keep your body white
In rainfall at morning and dewfall at night.

And this shall be for music
when no one else is near,
The fine song for singing,
the rare song to hear!
That only I remember,
that only you admire,
Of the broad road that
stretches and the
roadside fire.
Robert Louis Stevenson

Sweet and Low

Sweet and low, sweet and low,
Wind of the western sea,
Low, low, breathe and blow,
Wind of the western sea!
Over the rolling waters go,
Come from the dying moon, and blow,
Blow him again to me;
While my little one, while my pretty one sleeps.

Sleep and rest, sleep and rest,
Father will come to thee soon;
Rest, rest, on mother's breast,
Father will come to thee soon;
Father will come to his babe in the nest,
Silver sails all out of the west
Under the silver moon;
Sleep, my little one, sleep, my pretty one, sleep.
Alfred, Lord Tennyson

Poem in Prose

This poem is for my wife
I have made it plainly and honestly
The mark is on it
Like the burl on the knife

I have not made it for praise
She has no more need for praise
Than summer has
On the bright days

In all that becomes a woman
Her words and her ways are beautiful
Love's lovely duty
The well-swept room

Wherever she is there is sun
And time and a sweet air
Peace is there
Work done

There are always curtains and flowers
And candles and baked bread
And a cloth spread
And a clean house

Her voice when she sings is a voice
At dawn by a freshening sea
Where the wave leaps in the
Wind and rejoices

Wherever she is it is now
It is here where the apples are
Here in the stars
In the quick hour

The greatest and richest good—
My own life to live—
This she has given me
If giver could
Archibald MacLeish

A Cradle Song

Sleep, sleep, beauty bright,
Dreaming in the joys of night;
Sleep, sleep; in thy sleep
Little sorrows sit and weep.

Sweet babe, in thy face
Soft desires I can trace,
Secret joys and secret smiles,
Little pretty infant wiles.

As thy softest limbs I feel
Smiles as of the morning steal
O'er thy cheek, and o'er thy breast
Where thy little heart doth rest.

O the cunning wiles that creep
In thy little heart asleep!
When thy little heart doth wake,
Then the dreadful night shall break.

William Blake

I Remember, I Remember

I remember, I remember,
The house where I was born,
The little window where the sun
Came peeping in at morn;
He never came a wink too soon,
Nor brought too long a day,
But not, I often wish the night
Had borne my breath away!

I remember, I remember,
The roses, red and white,
The violets, and the lily cups,
Those flowers made of light!
The lilacs where the robin built,
And where my brother set
The laburnum on his birthday,—
The tree is living yet!

Thomas Hood

The Children's Hour

Between the dark and the daylight,
When the night is beginning to lower,
Comes a pause in the day's occupations,
That is known as the Children's Hour.

I hear in the chamber above me
The patter of little feet,
The sound of a door that is opened,
And voices soft and sweet.

From my study I see in the lamplight,
Descending the broad hall stair,
Grave Alice, and laughing Allegra,
And Edith with golden hair.

A whisper and then a silence:
Yet I know by their merry eyes
They are plotting and planning together
To take me by surprise.

A sudden rush from the stairway,
A sudden raid from the hall!
By three doors left unguarded
They enter my castle wall!

They climb up into my turret
O'er the arms and back of my chair;
If I try to escape, they surround me;
They seem to be everywhere.

They almost devour me with kisses.
Their arms about me entwine
Till I think of the Bishop of Bingen
In his Mouse-Tower on the Rhine!

Do you think, O blue-eyed banditti,
Because you have scaled the wall,
Such an old mustache as I am
Is not a match for you all!

I have you fast in my fortress,
And I will not let you depart,
But put you down into the dungeon
In the round-tower of my heart.

And there will I keep you forever,
Yes, forever and a day,
Till the walls shall crumble to ruin,
And moulder in dust away.
Henry Wadsworth Longfellow

The Blue Bowl Reward

All day I did the little things,
The little things that do not show;
I brought the kindling for the fire
I set the candles in a row,
I filled a bowl with marigolds,
The shallow bowl you love the best—
And made the house a pleasant place
Where weariness might take its rest.

The hours sped on, my eager feet
Could not keep pace with my desire.
So much to do, so little time!
I could not let my body tire;
Yet, when the coming of the night
Blotted the garden from my sight,
And on the narrow graveled walks
Between the guarding flower stalks
I heard your step; I was not through
With services I meant for you.

You came into the quiet room
That glowed enchanted with the bloom
Of yellow flame. I saw your face,
Illumined by the firelit space,
Slowly grow still and comforted—
"It's good to be home," you said.
Blanche Bane Kuder

The House By The Side Of The Road

There are hermit souls that live withdrawn
In the peace of their self-content;
There are souls, like stars, that dwell apart
In a fellowless firmament;
There are pioneer souls that blaze their paths
Where highways never ran—
But let me live by the side of the road
And be a friend to man.

Let me live in a house by the side of the road,
Where the race of men go by—
The men who are good and the men who are bad,
As good and as bad as I.
I would not sit in the scorner's seat,
Or hurl the cynic's ban—
Let me live in a house by the side of the road,
And be a friend to man.

I see from my house by the side of the road,
By the side of the highway of life,
The men who press with the ardor of hope
The men who are faint with the strife.

But I turn not away from their smiles nor their tears—
Both parts of an infinite plan—
Let me live in a house by the side of the road
And be a friend to man.

I know there are brook-gladdened meadows ahead
And mountains of wearisome height;
And the road passes on through the long afternoon
And stretches away to the night.
But still I rejoice when the travelers rejoice,
And weep with the strangers that moan,
Nor live in my house by the side of the road
Like a man who dwells alone.

Let me live in my house by the side of the road
Where the race of men go by—
They are good, they are bad, they are weak, they are
strong,
Wise, foolish—so am I.
They why should I sit in the scorner's seat
Or hurl the cynic's ban?
Let me live in my house by the side of the road
And be a friend to man.

Sam Walter Foss

A Wonderful Mother

God made a wonderful mother,
A mother who never grows old;
He made her smile of the sunshine,
And He molded her heart of pure gold;
In her eyes He placed bright shining stars,
On her cheeks, fair roses you see;
God made a wonderful mother,
And He gave that dear mother to me.

Pat O'Reilly

To My Son

I will not say to you, "This is the way; walk in it."
For I do not know your way or where the Spirit may call
you. It may be to paths I have never trod or ships on the
sea leading to unimagined lands afar, Or haply, to a star!

Or yet again Through dark and perilous places racked
with pain and full of fear. Your road may lead you far
away from me or near—I cannot guess or guide, but
only stand aside.

Just this I say: I know for every truth there is a way for
each to walk, a right for each to choose, a truth to use.
And though you wander far, your soul will know that true
path when you find it. Therefore, go!

I will fear nothing for you day or night! I will not grieve
at all because your light is called by some new name; Truth
is the same! It matters nothing to call it star or sun—
All light is one.
Author Unknown

Life's Lessons

I learn, as the years roll onward
And leave the past behind,
That much I had counted sorrow
But proves that God is kind;
That many a flower I had longed for
Had hidden a thorn of pain,
And many a rugged bypath
Led to fields of ripened grain.

The clouds that cover the sunshine
They cannot banish the sun;
And the earth shines out the brighter
When the weary rain is done.
We must stand in the deepest shadow
To see the clearest light;
And often through wrong's own darkness
Comes the very strength of light.

The sweetest rest is at even
After a wearisome day,
When the heavy burden of labor
Has borne from our hearts away;

And those who have never known sorrow
Cannot know the infinite peace
That falls on the troubled spirit
When it sees at least release.

We must live through the dreary winter
If we would value the spring;
And the woods must be cold and silent
Before the robins sing.
The flowers must be buried in darkness
Before they can bud and bloom,
And the sweetest, warmest sunshine
Comes after the storm and gloom.
Author Unknown

When I Have Time

When I have time so many things I'll do
To make life happier and more fair
For those whose lives are crowded now with care;
I'll help to lift them from their low despair
When I have time.

When I have time the friend I love so well
Shall know no more these weary, toiling days;
I'll lead her feet in pleasant paths always
And cheer her heart with words of sweetest praise,
When I have time.

When you have time! The friend you hold so dear
May be beyond the reach of all your sweet intent;
May never know that you so kindly meant
To fill her life with sweet content
when you had time.

Now is the time! Ah, friend, no longer wait
To scatter loving smiles and words of cheer
To those around whose lives are now so dreary
They may not need you in the coming year
Now is the time!

Author Unknown

Social Studies

Woody says, "Let's make our soap,
It's easy.
We learned about it
in school."
He told Mother,
"All you do is
Take a barrel.
Bore holes in the sides,
And fill it with straw.
Ashes on top-"

"No," said Mother.
Mary Neville

Apology For Youth

Stand at my window;
watch them pass;
a lass and a lad,
a lad and a lass.

This is a way
to go to school,
learning an olden,
golden rule.

They seek for wisdom
in a book;
then they look up
and look—and look.

And wonder, wonder
if, after all,
wisdom is so
reciprocal.

They ask for beauty,
ask for truth
who have no thought
to ask for youth.

Theirs are the earth,
the sea, the sky;
they sing; they dance,
they float; they fly.

Why do they hurry,
hurry so?
Can they or will they
or do they know

They will earn some love;
they will learn some truth,
but never learn nor earn back youth.

Stand at my window,
lad and lass;
let not this youth,
this young love pass.

Hold the wonder;
love the lore
you would one day change
the slow years for.

Sister M. Madeleva, C.S.C.

Child's Evening Hymn

Now the day is over,
Night is drawing nigh,
Shadows of the evening
Steal across the sky.

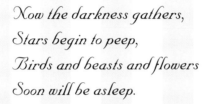

Now the darkness gathers,
Stars begin to peep,
Birds and beasts and flowers
Soon will be asleep.

Jesus give the weary
Calm and sweet repose,
With thy tenderest blessing
May our eyelids close.

Grant to little children
Visions bright of thee,
Guard the sailors tossing
On the deep blue sea.

Comfort every sufferer
Watching late in pain;
Those who plan some evil
From their sin restrain.

Through the long night-watches
May thy angels spread
Their white wings above me,
Watching round my bed.

When the morning wakens,
Then may I arise
Pure and fresh and sinless
In thy holy eyes.
Sabine Baring-Gould

Edgar A. Guest Considers "The Old Woman Who Lived in A Shoe" and the Good Old Truths Simultaneously

It takes a heap o' children to make a home
that's true, And home can be a palace grand
or just a plain, old shoe;

But if it has a mother dear and a good old dad
or two, Why that's the sort of good old home for
good old me and you.

Of all the institutions this side the Vale
of Rest. Howe'er it be it seems to me a good
old mother's best;

And fathers are a blessing, too, they give
the place a tone; In fact each child should try
to have some parents of his own.

The food can be quite simple; just a sop of
milk and bread. Are plenty when the kiddies
know it's time to go to bed.

And every little sleepy-head will dream
about the day When he can go to work because
a Man's Work is his Play.

And, oh, how sweet his life will seem, with naught
to make him cross, And he will never watch the
clock and always mind the boss.

And when he thinks (as may occur), this
thought will please him best; That ninety million
think the same—including Eddie Guest.
Louis Untermeyer

Nancy Hanks

If Nancy Hanks
Came back as a ghost,
Seeking news
Of what she loved most,
She'd ask first,
"Where's my son?
What's happened to Abe?
What's he done?
"Poor little Abe,
Left all alone
Except for Tom,

Who's a rolling stone;
He was only nine
The year I died.
I remember still
How hard he cried.

"Scraping along
In a little shack
With hardly a shirt
To cover his back,
And a prairie wind
To blow him down,
Or pinching times
If he went to town.

"You wouldn't know
About my son?
Did he grow tall?
Did he have fun?
Did he learn to read?
Did he get to town?
Do you know his name?
Did he get on?"

Rosemary Benet

Acknowledgments

The compiler and publisher have made every effort to trace the ownership of all copyrighted poems. While expressing regret for any error unintentionally made, the publisher will be pleased to make the necessary correction in future editions of the book.

Sincere thanks are due to the following publishers for cooperation in allowing the use of poems selected from their publications:

"A Cradle Song" by W.B. Yeats. Reprinted with the permission of Scribner, a division of Simon & Schuster from *The Collected Works of W. B. Yeats, Volume I: The Poems*, revised and edited by Richard J. Finneran. Copyright © 1983, 1989 by Anne Yeats.

"Apology for Youth" by Sister M. Madeleva, C.S.C., from *The Four Last Things*, copyright 1923, 1927, 1935, 1936, 1938, 1941, 1946, 1951, 1954, 1955, 1958, 1959 by Sister M. Madeleva, C.S.C. Copyright renewed 1951, 1955 by Sister M. Madeleva, C.S.C. Reprinted by permission of The Congregation of the Sisters of the Holy Cross.

"Edgar A. Guest Considers 'The Good Old Woman Who Lived in a Shoe' and The Good Old Truths Simultaneously" from *Selected Poems and Parodies* by Louis Untermeyer, copyright 1935 by Harcourt Brace & Company and renewed 1962 by Louis Untermeyer, reprinted by permission of the publisher.

"In an Iridescent Time" by Ruth Stone. First published in *The New Yorker* (under the title "Laundry"), copyright © 1958 by Ruth Stone. Reprinted by permission of Ruth Stone.

"Nancy Hanks" by Rosemary Benet from *A Book of Americans* by Rosemary and Stephen Vincent Benet. Copyright © 1933 by Rosemary and Stephen Vincent Benet. Copyright renewed © 1961 by Rosemary Carr Benet. Reprinted by permission of Brandt & Brandt Literary Agents, Inc.